Date Due

CAT. NO 24 162   PRINTED IN U.S.A.   BRO DART

ALEX HALEY

Sylvia B. Williams

Published by Abdo & Daughters, 4940 Viking Drive, Suite 622, Edina, Minnesota 55435.

Copyright © 1996 by Abdo Consulting Group, Inc., Pentagon Tower, P.O. Box 36036, Minneapolis, Minnesota 55435 USA. International copyrights reserved in all countries. No part of this book may be reproduced in any form without written permission from the publisher.

Printed in the United States.

Cover Photo credit: Wide World Photos
Interior Photo credits: Wide World Photos, pages 6, 12, 14, 18, 23
Archive Photos, pages 5, 11, 17, 21, 27

Edited by Julie Berg

Library of Congress Cataloging-in-Publication Data

Williams, Sylvia B.
    Alex Haley / Sylvia B. Williams: (edited by Jill Wheeler).
    p. cm. -- (I have a dream)
    Includes bibliographical references (p. 31) and index.
    ISBN 1-56239-570-X
1. Haley, Alex--Juvenile literature. 2. Historians--United States--Biography--Juvenile literature. 3. Afro-American Historians--Biography--Juvenile literature. I. Wheeler, Jill C., 1964-   II. Series.
E175.5.H27W55   1996
813'.54--dc20
[B]   95-41610
                                                         CIP
                                                         AC

TABLE OF CONTENTS

Chapter 1

The

Roots

of

Survival

GRANDMOTHER'S STORY

*A*lex Haley published only two major works in his career, but those works reached millions of people and greatly affected American society. His story of a family's love and survival sparked pride among African Americans and helped them understand and appreciate their special heritage. White people better understood the role of slavery in America's history. People of all races were stirred to take another look at their links with the past. The stories told to Haley by his grandmother and her sisters led him to trace his family's roots back several generations into Africa.

As a young boy, Alex loved sitting on the front porch at his grandmother's house listening to her tell stories with her sisters. Every evening after supper, the women would sit in their rocking chairs and tell stories that had been handed down from the days of slavery.

Alex Haley published two major books in his career,
Roots *and* Malcolm X.

A SLAVE NAMED TOBY

*T*he stories Alex most liked to hear were about his ancestor, Kunta "Kinte" (KIN-tay), who had come from Africa many years before. Kinte was brought to Virginia as a slave to live on a plantation. He insisted on being called "Kinte" rather than his slave name "Toby." He married and had a daughter named Kizzy.

Author Alex Haley on the set of Roots, *a 12-hour television mini-series.*

Kinte spent many hours telling Kizzy how he had been captured by slave traders one day when he was cutting wood to make a drum. He also taught her words from his native tongue, calling a guitar a "ko" and a river "kamby bolongo." He told her stories about his people and his country that he had left behind.

CHICKEN GEORGE

Kinte was crushed when Kizzy, his only child, was sold to another plantation at age 16. When Kizzy grew up, she had a son named George. Of all of Alex's ancestors, George was probably the most famous. He became a well-known gamecock trainer (training roosters to fight each other in a contest) and received the nickname "Chicken George."

George was the father of eight children. He loved telling them the stories his mother had told him. Each time one of his children was born, he would gather them all together and tell again the story of their African great-grandfather Kinte and their grandmother Kizzy.

The story continued on through Tom, George's fourth son. Tom also had eight children, the youngest a daughter named Cynthia. Cynthia was two years old when her father, Tom, and grandfather, George, led a wagontrain of freed slaves to Henning, Tennessee. At this point in the story, Alex was always fascinated when he heard about Cynthia, his grandmother—the one who sat right there on the front porch. The one who had told this same story to him.

These stories were passed down to children and grandchildren without fail. Each following generation would pass the information on to the next generation. This family history was passed down a total of seven generations.

This history gave Alex Haley the basic information that made it possible for him to trace his genealogy, all the way back to Africa.

A SECURE CHILDHOOD

Alex Palmer Haley was born in Ithaca, New York, on August 11, 1921. His parents were Simon and Bertha Haley. His father was a college professor who taught agriculture. His mother, also a teacher, was gifted musically.

When Alex was a tiny baby, he and his mother came to stay with his grandparents while his father finished his education. His grandparents lived in Henning, a small town in west Tennessee.

Alex became the son his grandfather had always wanted. Before he even started to talk, his grandfather carried him along with him wherever he went. He even took him along when he went to work.

His grandfather owned a lumber company. It was very unusual in those days for an African American to own a business. But when the white owner got deeply in debt, the bank president offered it to Alex's grandfather rather than shutting it down. The house his grandfather built was one of the finest in Henning.

Alex loved to play at the lumber company while his grandfather worked. He especially liked to spin around in his grandfather's chair. He would turn around and around until he got dizzy. He also enjoyed playing on the stacks of lumber, where his imagination took him on many exciting adventures.

Alex was five years old when his grandfather died. For a while, the little boy felt that his whole world had ended. His grandmother understood how much the small boy missed his close companion. So she spent hours with him trying to fill the empty spot in his heart that his grandfather had left. She and Alex became very close.

ALEX MEETS A GREAT SCIENTIST

Alex's two younger brothers, George and Julius, have also been successful in their chosen careers. George, a lawyer, is chief counsel to the United States Information Agency. Julius became a United States Navy Department Architect.

One morning when Alex, George, and Julius were young, their father told them, "There is someone special I want you to meet." They drove to the Tuskegee Institute in Alabama. Simon introduced them to the great scientist, George Washington Carver. They visited his research laboratory and he talked to them about studying hard in school. As they were leaving, Carver gave Alex a flower.

MOVING FROM TOWN TO TOWN

After finishing his education, Simon came back home to run the lumber company. Bertha taught school. Later, the lumber company was sold. Alex and his family moved to different college towns, where his father worked as a professor.

The Haley's lived in Normal, Alabama, for a long period of time, where Simon taught at A & M College. However, Alex and his brothers always spent the summers in Tennessee with their grandmother.

George Washington Carver in his research laboratory.

A GREAT LOSS

*W*hen Alex was 10 years old, his mother died. This was a difficult time for Alex and his younger brothers. Their father did his best to give them extra love and attention.

Simon later remarried, to Zeona Hatcher, also a college professor. They had a baby girl named Lois. Having a sister at the Haley house was quite an adjustment for the three Haley brothers.

Alex graduated from high school at the early age of fifteen. He then attended Elizabeth City Teachers College in North Carolina for two years.

Alex Haley (left) with his son William and grandson William Alexander, Jr.

Chapter **2**

From

Messboy

to

Writer

*A*t the age of seventeen, Alex joined the United States Coast Guard as a messboy. A messboy helps the cook and does kitchen chores. He later worked as the ship's cook.

When Alex went to sea, he took a portable typewriter, one of his prized possessions. His father had insisted that he learn to type when he was in high school. He used his typewriter to write letters for his shipmates. They paid him one dollar per letter.

While at sea, Alex spent many hours reading, a favorite pastime since he was very young. One day the idea struck him to write his own stories. It amazed him that he could roll a blank sheet of paper into his typewriter and write something that other people would read.

Alex Haley, Chief Journalist for the U.S. Coast Guard, 1949.

Alex loved the water and wrote adventure stories about the sea. Many of the stories came from United States naval records. He worked hard on his writing, but it was eight years before he sold his first story to a men's adventure magazine.

When Pearl Harbor was attacked by Japan and World War II started, Alex was serving on a U.S. Coast Guard patrol ship stationed at New Bern, North Carolina. He, like most Americans, was horrified that something like this could happen.

Later, he was transferred to a much larger cargo vessel, the *USS Murzim*. This ship carried 500-pound bombs to South Pacific airbases. One day Alex and his shipmates heard a terrific noise. They discovered that their sister ship, the *Serpens*, carrying the exact cargo they were carrying, had exploded. Only two people onboard during the explosion survived. Alex and his shipmates realized how close to death they were and that war was not a game.

After World War II, the Coast Guard created a special position just for him—Chief Journalist. Now he could use his writing skills on his job, handling public relations for the Coast Guard.

LIFE ON DRY LAND

*A*fter spending 17 years at sea, Alex retired from the Coast Guard. Alex never had any formal training in writing, but he was determined to write full-time.

Alex experienced failure many times before he started selling any stories. He often didn't even have a nickel in his pocket or any food in his cupboard, but he never gave up. He was determined to become a successful writer.

When Alex began writing full-time, he had help and support from a special childhood friend, George Sims. George found him a place to live and gave him food. He later helped him by doing research. They remained close friends through the years.

MALCOLM X

*E*ventually *Reader's Digest* magazine started giving Alex assignments to write biographies of famous people.

One of the people he interviewed and wrote about was Malcolm X, a spokesman for the Nation of Islam. Haley was asked by a publisher to write a book about Malcolm X, telling how Malcolm Little became Malcolm X. Alex spent a year talking intensely with Malcolm X and a year writing the book. It sold more than six million copies and became required reading for many high schools and colleges across America.

Shortly after the book was completed, Malcolm X was assassinated. He never got to read the book.

Malcolm X, leader of the black Muslim movement.

THEY'RE UP THERE WATCHING

*A*s Alex continued to write, the story his grandmother had told him about "Kinte" kept going through his mind. He decided to try to find out about his ancestor of long ago. He began reading every book he could find about African history.

Alex made a visit to see his cousin, Georgia. She was the only relative still living who had told family stories on the front porch. When Alex told her he wanted to find which African tribe Kinte had come from, she became very excited.

"You go ahead," she said. "Your grandma and all the others, they're up there watching!" Alex remembered what Cousin Georgia told him many times during his long search. This encouraged him not to give up.

Alex Haley on the set of Roots II *with Richard Thomas (left), David Wolper, and Henry Fonda.*

STARTING IN WASHINGTON, D.C.

*A*lex went to the National Archives Building in Washington, D.C. This building contains all of the family records for the United States. He discovered the names of his ancestors in official United States Government records. He had believed those stories his grandmother told. But to see the names of the people in those stories gave Alex an awesome feeling.

Next, he tried to discover which African language to which "Kinte" and the other "k" sounds belonged. He finally found an expert in African studies, Jan Vansina, who told him that these words were from the Mandinka language in Gambia, Africa.

Vansina was amazed to find that these few words had been so carefully preserved and handed down through the generations. It was hard for him to believe that Alex had heard the same African sounds many, many years later that Kizzy had first heard from Kinte.

Alex then was introduced to Ebou Manga from Gambia, who was studying in the United States. Alex explained about his search. Mangas was convinced his family back in Africa could be of help. So the two soon boarded a plane to Africa.

Chapter 3

In

Search

of

Kunta Kinte

In Juffre, a village in Gambia, Alex met with Ebou Manga's father and other men who were knowledgeable about Gambia's history. They told Alex about the "griots" who could still be found in back-country villages. Griots are elderly men who can recite the history of villages and families. Some of them can talk for three days without telling the same story.

Eventually Alex was able to meet a griot who knew about the Kinte clan. To do this he had to travel up the river he had heard about for so many years, the "Kamby Bolongo" (the Gambia River).

To travel into the heart of Gambia, Alex had to hire a launch to take him up the river and a lorry to carry supplies. He felt butterflies in his stomach as the launch eased out into the wide, swift river. But he was thrilled to gaze out onto the same river that Kinte must have traveled.

Alex arrived in the small back-country village of Juffure, from which Kinte had come. The village was still very much like it was 200 years before, with mud houses and thatched roofs. The villagers gathered with Alex as he listened to the griot tell about his ancestors down through the ages.

The griot told about when Kinte had gone off to chop wood and had been captured by slave traders. Alex could not believe his ears. He was hearing the same story he had heard on his grandmother's front porch when he was a boy. Kinte was actually Alex's great-great-great-great grandfather.

Gambia is a tiny, African country located inside Senegal. Kunta Kinte came from Juffure, a village in Gambia.

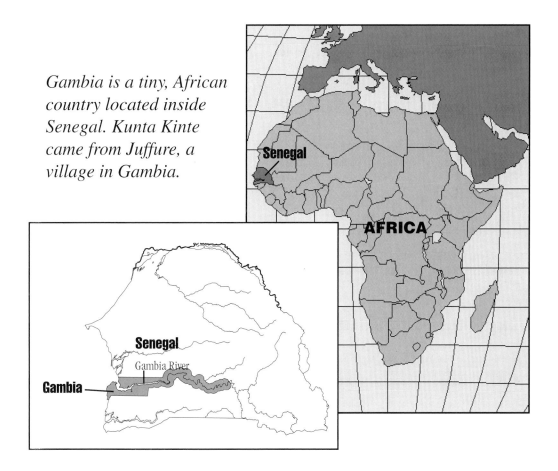

ONE OF THEIR OWN

*W*hen the villagers found out that Kinte was Alex's ancestor, they formed a ring around him and began chanting softly. One at a time, each mother placed her baby in Alex's arms. Alex later learned that he had taken part in an ancient ceremony. They had claimed him as one of their own.

When Alex was flying home from Africa, he decided to write a book. This book would tell the story of his ancestors, beginning with Kinte and ending with himself.

Alex went on to discover the slave ship that had brought Kinte to America. He found records showing that the American ship, *Lord Ligonier*, left Africa about the same time that Kinte was captured. It docked in Annapolis, Maryland. Kinte had always told the story of being brought by ship to "Naplis."

To understand the terror a slave must have felt crossing the ocean, Alex booked passage on a ship sailing from West Africa to the United States. Each night he would go down in the bottom part of the ship, strip to his underwear, and lie on a rough board. After that experience he understood better how Kinte must have felt traveling on the slave ship to a strange country.

A PULITZER PRIZE

Alex's search, from beginning to end, took 12 years. He had traveled over half-a-million miles and collected research from over 50 libraries. Alex began the difficult task of organizing all of the information he had collected.

Alex put all of his information into a book, *ROOTS: The Saga of an American Family*. Struck by the idea that *Roots* was completed in 1976, America's 200th birthday, Alex dedicated it as "a birthday offering to my country."

The book quickly became a bestseller and received many awards, including a special Pulitzer Prize. Over eight million copies have been sold, and has even been used as a textbook for teaching college courses.

Author Alex Haley (right), reads about himself winning the Pulitzer Prize for his book Roots. *With him are his brothers Julius (left) and George (center).*

...AND AN EMMY AWARD

*R*oots was made into a 12-hour television mini-series. In 1976, producers of this program were afraid that the American people would not accept a lengthy story about an African-American family. But they need not have worried. It became one of the most-watched television events of all time. It won several Emmy awards (the highest award for television), and is still being shown today on certain networks.

Because the mini-series was so popular, Alex was asked to write other programs just for television. They were called "Roots: The Next Generation" and "Roots: The Gift," a Christmas program.

Alex's determination paid-off. He completed the 12-year search that uncovered his family's roots. He completed the lengthy process of writing a book about his family's history spanning seven generations. He achieved success as an author and became well-known around the world.

Alex Haley on the set of Roots II, *1978.*

BACK TO HIS ROOTS

*A*lex became a millionaire overnight. He started his own business, The Kinte Corporation, and began producing films and records. He also became famous, and everywhere he went, people said, "There goes the Roots Man." To get away from crowds and have some privacy, he later bought a farm near Knoxville, Tennessee, and spent his last years there.

Alex wrote many articles for popular magazines, appeared on many television shows, and was a successful lecturer across the nation. He especially liked to speak to student groups. Rather than telling them how he wrote *Roots*, he would tell them what they were doing today affected the direction of their lives; that they needed to think carefully about what they were doing.

Alex was saddened that storytelling is a tradition no longer passed from generation to generation. He felt that today's children miss so much by not hearing their family history because storytelling was so important in his life.

Much of the money Alex made on *Roots* went for legal fees. Several writers accused him of copying their works. One charge was dropped, but the other cost him several hundred thousand dollars. Alex claimed his researchers gave him material without telling him where it was found.

Alex's own family consists of three children, William, Lydia Ann and Cynthia. Although he was divorced, he and his children remained close, and he followed the tradition of sharing the family stories with them. His son runs the business Alex started, now called The Haley Corporation.

One of the purposes of the Haley Corporation is to fund scholarships for students from Juffure, Gambia, to study in the United States. Money has also been given to the village school to help the children get a better education.

THE CHAPTER ENDS

*O*n February 10, 1992, a heart attack ended Alex Haley's life. He was 70 years old. Though his life is over, the impact he had on people and families of all races will not be forgotten. And the inspiration of his writings will live forever in the hearts of those they touched.

Alex had begun researching and writing about his father's family. This story, *Queen*, was completed and published after his death. He had plans to write a book describing the 12 years he spent searching for the records of his ancestors and the many miles he covered. Plans were also made to write a book about his hometown, Henning, Tennessee.

The family home in Henning, where Alex spent his childhood, has been turned into a museum. It is the first historic site in Tennessee that focuses entirely on African American heritage. In the back of his mind, Alex had always planned on going back to Henning to live the remainder of his life. His body is buried there, in the backyard of his boyhood home.

Author Alex Haley.

ROOTS GENEALOGY

KINTE
(Alex Haley's Great-Great-Great-Great Grandfather)
Born 1750 in Juffure, Gambia, Africa

KIZZY
(Alex Haley's Great-Great-Great-Grandmother)

GEORGE
(Alex Haley's Great-Great Grandfather)

TOM — 4TH SON
(Alex Haley's Great Grandfather)

CYNTHIA — 8TH CHILD
(Alex Haley's Grandmother)

BERTHA
(Alex Haley's Mother)

ALEX HALEY
Born 1921

GLOSSARY

Agriculture - business of raising crops or livestock.

Ancestor - one from whom person is descended.

Ancient ceremony - certain acts of times long past, performed for special occasions.

Assassinated - murdered, especially a public figure.

Biographies - stories about other people's lives.

Cargo - load of goods carried by ship.

Freed slaves - people who had been slaves that have been given their freedom.

Freighter - large ship used to carry goods.

Gamecock - rooster trained to fight another rooster in a contest.

Genealogy - record of ancestors in the order they were born.

Generation - group of people born at about the same time.

Griots - elderly African men who are tribe historians. They speak the history rather than write it.

Heritage - something passed down from ancestors.

Interview - meeting between a writer and a person from whom information is sought.

Laboratory - where scientific experiments are done.

Launch - open boat used to carry goods, used on a river.

Lorry - long flat wagon used to carry goods on land.

Mandinka - tribe of people from Gambia, Africa.

Messboy - helps the cook on a ship with kitchen work.

Native tongue - language learned at birth from country where one is born.

Plantation - very large farm where crops such as cotton or tobacco are grown usually using slaves or unpaid workers.

Pulitzer Prize - special award given each year for journalism, literature, and music.

Publish - to produce printed materials for sale to public.

Research - looking for facts and information about a certain subject.

Slave traders - men who captured people from their village and sold them to be used as servants.

Slavery - the practice of forcing people to work for no pay.

Tradition - handing down beliefs, customs, or history from one generation to another.

BIBLIOGRAPHY

The Commercial Appeal. Memphis Publishing Company, Memphis, Tennessee.

Current Biography. H.W. Wilson Company, 1977.

Dictionary of Literary Biographies: *Afro-American Writers, Dramatists and Prose Writers.* Gale Research Company, Detroit, Michigan.

Haley, Alex. *Roots: The Saga of an American Family.* Dell Publishing Company, 1976.

Haley, Alex. "Why I Remember," *Parade Magazine*, December 1, 1991.

Masterpieces of African-American Literature. Harper-Collins, 1992.

INDEX